# Mindful thoughts for
# COOKS

First published in the UK and North America in 2018 by

*Leaping Hare Press*

An imprint of The Quarto Group
The Old Brewery, 6 Blundell Street
London N7 9BH, United Kingdom
**T** (0)20 7700 6700  **F** (0)20 7700 8066
www.QuartoKnows.com

British Library Cataloguing-in-Publication Data
A catalogue record for this book is available from the British Library

ISBN: 978-1-78240-623-5

This book was conceived, designed and produced by

*Leaping Hare Press*

58 West Street, Brighton BN1 2RA, UK

Publisher: *Susan Kelly*
Creative Director: *Michael Whitehead*
Editorial Director: *Tom Kitch*
Art Director: *James Lawrence*
Commissioning Editor: *Monica Perdoni*
Project Editor: *Stephanie Evans*
Illustrator: *Lehel Kovacs*

Printed in Slovenia by GPS Group

1  3  5  7  9  10  8  6  4  2

# Mindful thoughts for
# COOKS
## *Nourishing body & soul*

## **Julia Ponsonby**

Leaping Hare Press

# Contents

INTRODUCTION **Slow Food in a Fast World**          6

A Deep Culinary History          10

Connecting with Nature's Cycles          16

The Journey          22

Packaging and Unpackaging          28

The Art of Nurture          34

The Heart of Every Home          40

Tuning into Our Senses          46

The Peacock in the Kitchen          52

Healthy Eating          58

Flexibility          64

Celebration          70

Are We What We Eat?          76

Thinking About Gluten and Sugar          82

Treading the Sure-footed Path of Organic Farming  88

Reasoning with Seasoning  94

Mindful Eating, Mindful Mealtimes  100

Lifting the Lid on Superfoods  106

Whittling Down Paraphernalia  112

Sharpening Our Knives and Our Lives  118

Patience, the Most Important Ingredient of All  124

Thinking About Food Waste  130

Seeing the Perfect in the Imperfect  136

Embracing Thankfulness  142

The Joy of Cooking  148

The Final Garnish: Cultivating Simplicity  154

DEDICATION AND ACKNOWLEDGEMENTS  160

# Slow Food in a
# **Fast World**

Cooking is surely one of the most pleasurable activities we engage in on a daily basis. Or at least it should be! It is an activity that satisfies our need to 'do' at a practical level and offers a sensory and aesthetic challenge. It has the potential to be social: the preparation can be team work, the results shared. Making things to eat is one of those daily tasks that is perfect for developing a more 'mindful' approach to life. Cooking is easily within our grasp and ready to benefit from a dose of slowing down and a gentle regime of awareness-building. Whatever we cook, it will turn out better if it is prepared in the absence of stress and with time to ensure it is served perfectly cooked, appropriately warm and very tasty.

The relevance of bringing a mindful approach to everyday life is especially poignant because in a fast-paced world we rarely take time to reflect. Instead of enjoying each moment as it comes, memories of the past vie with concerns for the future. By dwelling on past hurts and grasping at the future we may undercut any sense of contentment with the present.

Cooks are very practical people – but not necessarily people who have much time for meditation or noticing their breath. Many chefs I know would laugh at the idea that bringing mindfulness into cooking could be a more important ingredient than, say, salt. Yet I am convinced that the most successful chefs are those who bring mindfulness into their cooking without even labelling it as such. Whether the activity of cooking attracts practical people, or an innate need to be practical draws people to engage in the process, does not matter. The fact is that cooking provides the ideal opportunity to disengage from the mental games that can ensnare our happiness and allows us to expand our repertoire of positivity. Letting our minds ripple out into consideration of everything that affects (and is affected by) what we cook introduces a broader element of identification, that goes beyond the cooking process. This enriches our moment and builds an overarching awareness into what we do.

The story of food today is critical to our well-being. It is as if we stand at a junction with a decision to make. Will we follow the path that leads up into the clouds, climbing a rainbow, along with the planes that import our food, or will we take the one that stays on the ground and reveals the fertile Earth to us? Is there a middle path? Nowadays, as part of a (not too) modern society, we are blessed with the opportunity to engage in our own food preparation, so we should celebrate this aspect of our food journey, grateful to have access to our own cooking facilities. The onus on who prepares food for whom has shifted in the past, and it is still shifting, so let's harvest the mindful experience that goes with the territory of being conscientious cooks while we can.

# A Deep
## Culinary History

What we do with food and where we get it from tells us a lot about our society and where it is going. The food we eat has been, and continues to be, formative in our physical and mental evolution.

Mindfulness is about living fully in the moment and extending that moment into the eternal domain of the soul. Connecting meaningfully with our human food story can also provide this sense of expanded awareness.

*Homo sapiens* are thought to have evolved from early hominids some 200,000 years ago and this may have had parallels with a coastal or riverside diet that fed the development of a larger brain, more akin to that of aquatic mammals than other apes. Such a diet would have included shellfish, fish and seaweed. In the more recent past, the introduction of grains that attended the dawn of agriculture fostered different lifestyles and, some would argue, different mental attributes. Fossil evidence suggests a deterioration of human health from this time (13,000-9,000 BCE) coinciding with a less nutrient-rich and more plant-based diet, with skeletal evidence of, for example, nutrition-related diseases such as osteoporosis.

## GLOBAL AND LOCAL

Fast-forwarding many thousands of years to the last century, a new cuisine has spread on the wide-spanning wings of globalization. This has allowed people around the world to connect with favourite classic meals from all corners of the Earth, turning these into international staples and overturning the concept of a diet based on traditions and locally sourced ingredients. Thus we have sushi, pasta, pizza and curries finding a comfortable nest in practically every country. Once upon a time, these 'food cuckoos' would have been seen as specialities, novel cuisines to be encountered almost exclusively in their countries of origin. Nowadays they can be enjoyed by almost anyone who experiences Western-style culture (wherever it pops up), creating common threads between diverse people.

At one level, we tread in the culinary paths of our ancestors when we make a favourite recipe that has been handed down in our family for generations of grandmothers; at another level, we walk the path of our international ancestry as we learn to perfect a pizza or a curry. Both the international and the personal hold a food message about our culture today and the way it has, on the one hand, become globalized and, on the other, still pulls us back to our roots because it has the power to rekindle old memories of nurture as well as evoke new pathways of opportunity. Thus we have the comfortable 'holding' value of food versus the exciting 'transcendental' aspect of what we eat vying for our attention in the modern world.

It can be fun to juggle with both. Indeed, the Californian-style 'fusion' food that I learned to cook when I first came to Schumacher College included an exciting mix of ingredients and flavours sourced from all over the world. I remember one salad that contained bananas, mayonnaise, raisins and cauliflower. These menus were a far cry from the seasonal local palette I try to work with now but there was within them an open embracing of difference and a willingness to experiment, be flexible and enter into the domain of innovation that synchs with the birth of a new enterprise.

Foods often carry with them the power to rekindle memories. Once I was given a delicious gluten-free recipe for a Polish walnut cake by a student called Sonja. Along with the recipe, she recounted the story of her family journeying out of war-torn Poland. It was a treacherous journey for her parents and grandparents. They had virtually nothing concrete of their former existence to hold on to, yet throughout the journey, some favourite recipes stayed firmly glued in their memories, ready to be recreated once safety was reached and home could be rebuilt. Many years later Sonja returned to her parents' part of Poland and found the same recipe being made; the familiar method and taste immediately acted as a culinary bridge that linked her into a homeland she could not remember in person. An echo of this can be found when our children leave home for the first time taking treasured recipes with them that help to build a bridge into their new lives – as well as adding a tasty measure of encouragement to their trips back home.

# Connecting with
# Nature's Cycles

Working with the seasons, we feel the alternating joys of renewal and reduced abundance as part of our human clock. Acknowledging the darkness, as well as the light, is part of what makes us tick. Wherever we find ourselves positioned on the planet Earth, wherever we find the place we call 'home' – this is where we will find our opportunity to experience the seasonal changes in nature's abundance, messaged to us in the form of different local produce as well as changing weather patterns. It is as if these vegetables, fruits, nuts or seeds are all speaking to us of the cosmos and our place in it. They are positioning us, and telling us where we are in the scheme of things in the very particular sense of place and of time. We and they are cycling around the Sun – though, the offspring of the plants and the trees are more closely coupled with the seasons of spring, summer, autumn and winter that hallmark a temperate climate, or the wet and dry season found at the Equator. The fruits that are offered up by nature as our food become a compass to these seasonal changes.

## A SENSE OF TIME AND PLACE

When we work with the seasons, we are engaging in more than just a process or style of cooking: we are engaging in a way of life and opening our eyes to the cycles of the cosmos around us. We are aligning ourselves with the natural cycles that bring the joys of renewal in the spring and the reality-hit of reduced abundance that corresponds with the coming of darkness in winter. As soon as we move away from linking our food with our place and the seasons of growth and renewal, we lose something. By moving into a domain of supermarket shopping in which everything we buy to cook and eat is illuminated by the bright electric lights of a huge store, we risk losing this connection with nature. Yes, we can buy strawberries during the winter months but what benefit is this if the taste is marred by the sense of weariness it evokes after a long journey encased in plastic? Better to hold our breath for the offerings of the new season when the unsurpassable taste of a freshly picked berry will quickly win us around to the virtues of local food – if we let it.

## PRESERVING TRADITIONS

And in between the seasons of abundance, we can appreciate the concentrated flavours of preserved foods. We may dry and salt our fish, curdle our milk for cheese, pickle our cabbage in vinegar, preserve our cherries in honey – and then relish these subtle flavours sitting together with bread made from grain that has been gathered and stored, then freshly milled to be turned into our daily bread.

This song of praise to the Earth's seasons may sound old-fashioned and idealized: today we have freezers to keep many vegetables fresh and to optimize their vitamin content, and we can use heated polytunnels to extend growing seasons. But if we keep seasonal ingredients as the archetypal backdrop for our life as a cook, there is no better way to ensure that what we cook will be optimum in flavour and deliciousness. There is no better way of imbuing ourselves with the rhythms of nature, which wrap around us whether we notice them or not.

Better the darkness we know and appreciate for its fecund mystery, its hibernating richness, than the darkness we despise and avoid as a form of blindness because we cannot see its place in the fullness of life, having been encouraged to skip over it by a modern lifestyle in which big shops create artificial food worlds. There is little beauty in eternal summers held under concrete roofs below skies where stars have been outshone by city lights. As cooks, the local patterning of abundance represented by the seasons is ours to reclaim, along with the stars and the moon.

# The
# Journey

How far have we travelled – and how far has our food travelled? When we see connections clearly, mindfulness is a tool for ecological and spiritual empowerment.

A journey is all about movement, and movement happens on many levels. True, we can endure the buffeting of long-distance travel as we run for a train, hop on a plane and feel the pressure change as we rise into the air and let ourselves endure dozens of hours of sitting still while being propelled to the other side of the world. Eventually, parched and tired we walk out into a new domain, letting new sounds, smells and sights shock our senses into full alert. We can recover but the experience costs us energy.

For a well-travelled fruit or vegetable, weariness from such a journey is expressed in the lack of nutritional vitality and brightness. Whereas we are revived by a good night's sleep and a good meal, it is hard to regain the lost potential of a food that has been picked under-ripe, deprived of sun and sent across the world in a fridge.

As psychological beings, we might also engage in a journey that involves no pretence at geographical travel at all. Rather, we could monitor our personal journey over the years of our life in terms of development from a needy child to a mature and forgiving adult, noting formative milestones along the way. In reality, true journeys of the soul usually combine an element of psychological and physical travel; the two go hand-in-hand with the psychological imperative to progress, seeking the physical movement of a journey in time and place to find its magic.

Discovery can happen at any time. Perhaps it is more likely you will experience a revelation if you go looking for it outside your comfort zone but sometimes it falls at your feet unexpectedly, like a ripe fruit from a tree.

One of the biggest revelations comes when we see a causal connection between one thing and another. We then have two realizations. First, that we have the power to follow this connection along from 'root to shoot', so we can see where the chain of connections is leading and predict what will happen next. Second, having seen a causal connection, we can often (though not always) break connections and redirect growth. This means that seeing connections clearly can give us agency, or power.

Moving to the example of food, when we are met with abundance of food in a supermarket and no knowledge of what it costs the environment to bring this food to us, we have no incentive and no reason not to buy it. But, how would it affect our actions if we knew more about this food in relation to its journey and the effect of this on the environment? Would our actions differ if we knew more about the consequences of our purchasing in terms of sustaining patterns of supply and demand?

This isn't a simple equation. The concept of 'food miles' (the distance food travels between its production and its consumption) was first coined by professor of food policy Tim Lang to highlight the dangers of long-distance food transport and the increase in carbon emissions it can cause. Within this equation, air travel generates more than one hundred times the carbon emissions of land or water travel. Furthermore, because the total carbon emissions in food production are often higher than those involved in its journey, eating local isn't always the most climate-friendly choice. So eating a tomato that has been grown locally but in a heated greenhouse may involve greater use of fossil fuel than importing a tomato from warmer climes where it was ripened naturally by the sun. What provides a more reliable guide is eating seasonally *and* locally, so both the intensive production methods and the long-distance transportation are avoided.

To make mindful decisions about purchasing fruit and veg in a shop, the key information we need to know is therefore origin (which gives us a measure in food miles) and mode of transport (which is indicative of the carbon footprint involved). This journey information will also give us the thumbs up (or down) when it comes to flavour, as no vegetable or fruit that has travelled long-distance or been produced hydroponically or under glass tastes anywhere as good as it could.

Piggy-backing on the concept of food miles, we now have the concept of waste miles, a term that describes the distance our discarded rubbish has to travel before it is either recycled or incinerated to produce energy. Much of this waste comes from food packaging. Both card and plastic may be dispatched to the other side of the world to be recycled. This secondary travel is a consideration we also need to bear in mind when we purchase heavily packaged food, so it is worth investigating the strategy of your local refuse disposal companies that deal with your waste. Then you will know what length of journey any packaging you buy may be embarking upon when you throw it away – and you'll discover what kind of environmental conscience your local authority and their waste disposal contractors have. Rubbish is big business nowadays, so we have every right to ask questions.

# Packaging
## and
# Unpackaging

---

What does it mean for food and for the planet when we package food – and do we sometimes over-package ourselves as well? Can we pare back to the essence and find out what really counts?

In the same way that our clothes and our homes protect us, so packaging protects food on its journey from wholesaler to retailer to consumer. Packaging not only protects and insulates, it also provides scope for advertising and conveying information about the contents, including nutritional advice and sell-by date. By the same token, the way we dress sends out a (sometimes quite literal) message about who we are. Could it be that, while putting words on a T-shirt and wearing it may appear to be a fashion statement or a political statement, it also suggests we are happy to turn ourselves into a commodity?

In nature, many foods are protected by an outer layer of skin or husk, and this is often all that is needed to keep fruit or vegetables clean and fresh on a supermarket shelf. The earliest added packaging took the form of natural materials that could be re-used and recycled, such as willow baskets, banana leaves and terracotta urns. However, for today's global consumer the packaging norm has escalated into elaborate plastic edifices that, when combined with colour-printed cardboard, metal and glass elements represent one sixth of our expenditure on food. Furthermore, food packaging in some countries now represents as much as one-third of all waste.

One of the most worrying examples of waste comes in the form of plastic, which reflects the proliferation of plastic products in the last seventy years. A shocking eight million tons of plastic waste is currently added annually to our precious ocean. In its most polluted places, plastic mass is six times the mass of plankton. One of the principal culprits is the plastic water bottle, which will take four hundred years to degrade in water and requires six times as much water to produce as a single bottle can hold. Non-biodegradable or very slowly degradable rubbish in the ocean, including land run-off in the form of agricultural chemicals, presents an enormous threat to marine life and water quality. Even without empathy for our fellow creatures of the sea, this is an issue for us land creatures too. Pollution makes its way back up the food chain and on to our plates.

As people who care about and value all life, we can by preference come to the deep realization that it is within our grasp to be part of a reduction in unnecessary use of plastics. For a moment, just visualize the amount of packaging that comes with every microwave meal, or even every portion of store prepared vegetables. Teaching ourselves and others to cook extends the benefit of self-sufficiency and removes the danger of becoming plastic-dependant, as well as enabling us to create healthier, fresher meals.

Pitted against the corporate agenda is the local food movement, which includes localized food distribution systems. It is in this (and the revival of home cooking that naturally flows from it) that there lies the greatest hope for a reduction of packaging. I can now buy local produce from a farmer's market once a week, and a zero-waste shop has opened in my town where people are encouraged to refill their containers of oil, beans, peanut butter, etc. It is a bit like going back to the 1950s, a moment in time before the food industry started to helter-skelter out of ecological balance. Even if such places aren't within your reach, you can still make some basic reductions: for instance avoiding single-use plastic in preference to ceramic, glass and metal beverage containers, and boiling tap water instead of using chemical sterilizers or bottled water. These are usually easy measures for us to take and, when collectively followed, such actions can have a big impact.

There are two other things that may stop the escalation of packaging in its tracks. One is the decline in the finite reserves of the fossil oil that is used to make plastic packaging, and the other is a taxation system that places the cost of waste squarely on the shoulders of both consumers and producers, thus building in an incentive to create and accept packaging that does no more than is necessary to safely protect products over minimum journeys. Be alert to who you support politically: the power to take such wise measures is in their hands.

When packaging becomes more valuable and more energy-intensive than the contents, then, it seems to me, something has gone seriously wrong. Likewise, when we allow ourselves to become objectified to the extent that we need frequent new 'disposable packaging' on our person, our attitude to ourselves is also part of the problem. Identifying the removal of true personal freedom that comes with any dependency, perceived or real, will allow us to begin addressing the problem and rebuilding a more mindful relationship to our natural resources.

# The Art of
# Nurture

Cooking offers us the opportunity to practise the nourishment of ourselves and others.

Let's make it easy – as easy as possible – for us to show ourselves for who we are. In the security of our own homes, let's do what we can to support the flowering of the person we feel ourselves to truly be, rather than the person we feel others think we ought to be. Let's forget about the way we present ourselves and get down to nurturing our soul.

Whenever I grow fragile beansprouts, first soaking then carefully rinsing them over several days, I am reminded of our own tender shoots. The initial overnight soak in water seems akin to time spent in the womb.

A miraculous germination begins: the forces of life are being activated. Later, the daily careful rinsing could be similar to the time when we learned to walk and talk, sometimes falling and stumbling over words. As those tiny squiggles emerge as roots, I have an appreciation that, although great care must be taken at all times, when this is granted there is also room in nature for a little rough-and-tumble, as there is in the development of any life. It's not that this gives us license to be rough, but rather that our kindness will often (and perhaps usually) be met halfway. What I mean to say is that a sustaining life force manifests itself before us as an expression, not only of our own nurturing but of a general life-loving phenomenon that permeates all existence.

## CULTIVATING GOOD PRACTICE

The art of nourishing begins with an understanding that healthy soil promotes the growth of healthy food, and a healthy ambience for serving up the food also contributes to the benefit of the food once it has been cooked. This could mean going to the market and selecting the most appealing vegetables while chatting to the stall holder about the farm and its growing practices. It could mean planting, tending and harvesting your own vegetables and preparing them from scratch, rejecting anything that looks damaged or inferior and developing a clear understanding of the correlation between good produce and good flavour. It could also mean selecting the best organic vegetables in a supermarket – and even if these were not available, the mindful cook could select the best of anything on offer and transform it into a satisfying meal. The next stage, the cooking, would be especially vital, as there might be a need to compensate for a lack of flavour that can be a reflection of nutritional poverty if less wholesome produce has been used.

When it comes to serving up the food that nourishes, a familiar environment imbued with the warmth of loved ones may be the best ambience. Equally, though, imagine yourself arriving at the end of a long and arduous pilgrimage to be welcomed by complete strangers with bowls of warm soup. You might never have been in such a home as theirs before, you might never have smelled such a soup, yet their beaming, friendly eyes and keenness to help might lead you to feel the replenishing nurture of the warm food reviving you. For once, you might put aside any thoughts of whether this food was made with ingredients you approve of and think only of your body's need for nourishment and the obvious health and goodwill of those looking after you. So why not try cooking a recipe that engages you in this transformative journey?

## SIMPLE NOURISHMENT

As an example of nurturing, people often recount childhood memories of being given a favourite food by a loved one when ill. My husband talks about the chicken soup his Auntie Hunca made him – a semi-transparent broth bobbing with bits of chicken, carrot, onion, potato and rice. I have many times sought to make this for him, buying organic chicken, organic carrots, onions, etc. To ensure the vitamins and minerals in the vegetables are kept to a maximum (as well as the flavour), I leave the skins on the vegetables. Although I am a vegetarian myself, I simmer the bones of the chicken to make a broth, thanking this bird for giving its life for us and glad in the knowledge that it will have had a good life, because animal welfare is one of the central tenets of an organic food production system. When the broth is ready, I combine it with the vegetables and chicken all the time thinking how much good this meal will bring. It is wonderful how happy this simple soup makes my husband and how he says he can feel it doing him good. I believe, if we gather together the elements that will combine to form a new whole, we can create a deliciousness greater than the sum of its parts.

# The **Heart** of Every **Home**

It is natural for the kitchen-dining rooms of today to become the heart of every home as we recognize the interdependence of the nurture of our bodies with the nurture of our spirit.

Throughout prehistory, the home was a single large space – perhaps a cave, a hut, or, for nomadic people, a yurt or tipi. The space was used for eating, sleeping and socializing, and had the hearth at its centre, often positioned so the smoke would be funnelled up through a space into the open air. This form continued as a main home structure for thousands of years, and is a tradition which is still evidenced in many parts of the rural, non-industrialized world.

Fast forwarding to the mid-1800s, in most industrialized countries, kitchens were utilitarian work spaces, a role they continued to hold until at least the 1950s. For wealthy families living in large residences, kitchens were often tucked away 'below stairs' or located at the back where produce could keep cool. Dining rooms were where all the more highbrow conversation happened. This pattern of use spread out from Europe to America, Australia and other countries where Europeans emigrated. But even in the eras before the kitchen became chic, as it is often considered today, this room had one important ingredient that lay at its centre, priming it for its future role as the heart of our homes. The kitchen had a hearth – a fire – a place where food could cook, and people and animals could keep warm. It is this essential and symbolic ingredient that holds the key to the power of the kitchen. In ancient Greece we find the mythological and archetypal precedent for this in the form of the goddess of the domestic realm, Hestia and her important role as the guardian of the fire at the heart of Olympus. This eternal flame symbolized life and nurture: anyone who came to sit by this fire would keep warm and be protected. No stranger would be turned away. Thus we find the notion that inclusivity is an important aspect of kitchens – something often missing from the strictly invited guests-only aura of dining rooms.

## A SENSE OF CONNECTION

But let's not forget that if the hearth is to be our guide to the heart of any home, then it must also be significant that lots of the cooking and eating also traditionally took place outside, as it still does when barbecues or field kitchens are set up. Perhaps the mobile hearth, associated with cooking and feasting outdoors in warmer weather, is an important reminder of the direct connection we need to keep with our Eden. Even if we do not possess a garden of our own, we need to externalize and internalize the connection with the productive world of nature that serves us so bountifully, especially when treated respectfully and in tune with natural cycles. To this end, building a connection with a market garden, an allotment or even a windowsill pot of herbs deepens our relationship with what we cook. The heart – our heart – is a place where depth of emotion is felt. Thus, to be cooking with a wide appreciation of the broader context of our sustenance feeds this capacity for deep understanding and burnishes our sense of the kitchen as the heart of our home.

The contemporary model of the kitchen that combines cooking with socializing and eating, without isolating or functionalizing the person (or people) who cook, brings the modern kitchen full circle, returning it the multi-purpose role it had in prehistoric times. Nowadays kitchen-living rooms typically include a child writing their homework at one end of a table, the politics of the day being debated at the other, and plenty of cooking happening in between. A skilful cook can quickly seize the opportunity to get ardent talkers to do a bit of nut-cracking or peeling at the same time, but do be careful. The mindful and safe use of a knife is better practised with as little distraction as possible, and sometimes a safer task like podding peas is better given to someone whose mind is elsewhere.

A kitchen is like a living organism: sometimes calm, sometimes busy, sometimes resting, sometimes digesting or ruminating. At one moment it is a debating chamber, at another a place for counselling, for making healing potions, or for sipping a hot drink. By allowing and encouraging our kitchens to become the true heart of our homes, while our organic gardens and fields become the blood they pump, we are moving forward in a truly positive direction, hand-in-hand with progress towards a happier and healthier existence. This is what it means to put warmth, nurture, sharing and generosity at the centre of your everyday lived experience.

# Tuning Into
# Our Senses

When we cook, we are given the opportunity to delight in a whole array not only of tastes, but smells, visual appeal, textures, and sounds.

Opportunities for using our senses crop up during the adventure of our meal preparation as we move from hedgerow, garden, kitchen and hob to table. Like an artist, we can work with a rich and varied palette of colours, flavours and textures. This in turn helps us reconnect with and utilize our intuitive and instinctive knowing.

We learn from an early age to identify the basic flavour sensations – but where does ginger lie on the spectrum of spicy? Is garlic hot? Why do some people love chilli while others cough, sweat and splutter?

Modern scientific research suggests that all our taste buds are able to taste the four traditional categories of sweet, sour, salt and bitter, and furthermore there is a fifth flavour commonly described using the Japanese term 'umami', which refers to a uniquely satisfying savoury taste sometimes equated with 'meatiness' or 'cheesiness'. Umami was first identified in 1907 by a Japanese scientist Kikunae Ikeda as a result of his work on the 'dashi' taste in the seaweed kombu. Ikeda found the flavour to be linked to a substance called ajinomoto, which was later identified as monosodium glutamate (MSG). While artificial MSG is an over-used additive, let's not forget that umami itself is a savoury flavour we can find in many wholesome foods.

## A FEAST FOR THE SENSES

The five basic tastes are not the whole story, though. Other factors include smell, texture, temperature, 'coolness' (such as of menthol) and 'hotness' (pungency) Aroma is often what draws us to food and gives us an appetite. Delicious smell is often the phenomenon that gets us salivating. Even people who don't drink coffee often inhale the sumptuous aromas of other people's brews; even those who profess to be gluten free can nonetheless be drawn by the wafting aromas of fresh bread baking in the oven. Likewise, appearance of food captivates our attention ahead of any mouthfuls, which is why chefs strive to present their food attractively. But there is more to it than simply good looks. The colour of fruit and vegetables is an indication of their different nutritional profiles, and by eating a varied diet we benefit from the array of phytonutrients they provide. There are sounds, too, that build the anticipation as we slice, stir and sizzle. Texture, such as crispness, chewiness and crunchiness, also adds to the overall pleasure of the eating experience.

The magic of taste is that it is both functional and gastronomic. Our ability to detect sweetness may originate from our need to consume energy-rich high carbohydrate foods, while our ability to detect salt reflects our need for an essential vibrant nutrient. Bitter, meanwhile, at its extreme, warns us of something that is potentially harmful or poisonous such as a toxic leaf in a hedgerow. However, in the middle ground there exists a playing field for gastronomy where the most wonderful and unique combinations lie. In this way we can not only evolve flavour but redress any imbalances we may inadvertently find: for example if food is too salty, we can increase the sour or sweet component to compensate for this.

Taking this as a parallel for consciousness generally, we can meditate on the need to find balance in our experience of good and bad, inviting happy thoughts to balance sad ones. We should not, however, deny the back notes of bitterness that tap at our awareness. Rather, in the name of wholeness, we need to acknowledge and allow the bitter and the sour feelings to be tasted fully – even those that make us wince. Consideration of something as immediately appealing and accessible as flavour development gives us confidence in the participatory nature of revitalizing our 'mojo' at all levels.

The most important thing about tuning into our senses is, then, to do just that. We must never lose touch with the raw experience of taste. Chefs and wine tasters may use flavour wheels to analyse, communicate and tease out the uniqueness of a flavour. For most people, it is enough to experience the amazing and myriad flavours that arrive in our mouth and relish the adventure of taste it takes us on. Sometimes, if we're lucky, this may lead us to taste the unique flavour of a place on the tips of our tongues as many wine lovers claim to. This experience is encapsulated by the French concept of 'terroir', which evokes a link between the terrain of a particular region and the nurturing influence of its environment, soils, climate and all the distinct life forces that influence the flavours of what grows in that place.

# The Peacock
## in the Kitchen

Developing attention to detail can reveal to us how much of life we normally don't notice – and this in turn makes us aware of the huge wealth of beauty that can be lost to us, yet is also ours to regain.

Although, as a cook, my number one priority is always for food to taste really good, I also appreciate times when there is no need to rush and careful attention can be given to the way things look. This involves not only the appearance of the individual edible components of a meal but the way everything is arranged together and the careful selection of the serving platters, bowls or dishes used to bring the food to the table, creating a feast for our eyes.

## BUILDING ANTICIPATION

Preparing and arranging such a feast offers us the opportunity to engage in a fine-tuning of our attention to detail: as cooks we are also the artists offering up a display, much as the peacock fans his incredible tail for all to admire. For this not to be a mere seeking out of praise, the reminder that food is impermanent and will soon be devoured, or spoil, helps us avoid investing too much of our ego in the process of creating beautiful meals. Rather, we do this as a dedication to a process, in the same way that Tibetan Buddhist monks build intricate sand mandalas, only to brush them away when complete, demonstrating the ephemeral nature of life.

We can also make our attention to detail and our careful arranging of food a celebration of the work that both humans and nature have put into growing special ingredients, some of which may be scarce and in need of carefully stringing out like a necklace of pearls. I remember an occasion when we foraged dandelions, dipped them in batter and fried them in hot oil. When the time came to eat, there was scarcely enough for one per person, yet when laid carefully on a wooden board, the sight was a comical delight for all to share as batter-encrusted heads sat there like cushions, while tapering stalks waved in the air.

When it comes to serving dishes, I have a bit of a soft spot for ceramics. Perhaps it is fortunate that pottery tends to break every now and then, though I never fail to grieve the loss of an attractive plate or bowl. For me, a simple glazed plate, which may or may not be patterned, provides a real enhancement for serving any meal, and so I think of it as an essential. I don't want to serve lovingly handmade food from dishes that are mass-produced stainless steel or plastic, however practical, because it feels like a real lowering of the tone. By contrast, hand-crafted ceramics with a real natural beauty to them allows the beauty and deliciousness of the soon-to-be-devoured food to ripple out that little bit further into the room.

There is a real yet invigorating challenge that comes when we invite haute cuisine into the kitchen and aim to make food both beautiful and delicious through careful cooking, tasting and display. We need to make sure that our invited guests sample this feast at exactly the optimum moment to appreciate the food at its most delicious. Serving the meal at the right temperature, in the right sequence, and coordinating it with the arrival of the guests is all part of the training of a cordon bleu chef. Thank goodness we don't have to worry about this every day – but when we choose to, let's take it as an exercise in developing attention to detail. I once met a fellow who, annoyed by his peacocks displaying at his front door all the time, propped mirrors up against a tree so the peacocks would display in front of them, mistaking their reflection for another peacock. In the same way, beautiful food and its preparation could become tiresome if we had to eat it, prepare it and admire it every day. However, looked at from another perspective, if the peacock's fantastic but ungainly tail can be taken as an example of the 'handicap principle' in neo-Darwinian evolutionary theory (that is, the idea that grand plumage attracts mates because only the healthiest bird could afford to lavish so much energy on growing it), so perhaps our ability to create very beautiful displays of food shows our ability to go beyond the call of duty and persevere against all odds when we need to. We are making a visual display of our decision and ability to prioritize mindfulness. Rather than a vanity or an indulgence of leisure time, this can be seen (and done) as a conscious prioritization of the importance of setting aside time to do things slowly and carefully, and with an attention to detail from which arises beauty and a sense of reverence.

# Healthy
## Eating

How nutritionally literate do we need to be to maintain a healthy diet?

In a world where junk food is on offer in every corner shop, it is vital to have a clear understanding of what makes food good or bad for us. In the past, what was available corresponded with the same life-promoting diet we evolved with. We therefore could eat healthily without having to be nutritionally literate beyond knowing what was obviously poisonous. The situation today is quite different.

In my chosen career I now focus on nutrition, health and sustainability on a daily basis. My earliest introduction to healthy eating was at school, learning in a simplified way about different food groups and the need for a balanced diet. I remember a pie chart showing the percentage of carbohydrate, protein, fibre, fat and sugar we needed in our daily intake. (Sugar is, of course, a carbohydrate but one we specifically need less of than other complex carbs.)

What is most striking when looking at images that promote good health is that our diet needs to be about one third fruit and vegetables and one third carbohydrate. However, what may not be obvious from these fairly simplified categories is that some carbohydrates are better than others, and to have a truly wholesome diet we need to be eating complex, unrefined carbohydrates that include all the nutritional benefits of the skin and husk. This in turn points us in the direction of an organic diet, because the skin and husk is also the part that absorbs pesticide residues, making it better to peel vegetables and fruit that are not organic. This is another reason why mindfully cooking for ourselves is usually the healthiest option: we are in the driving seat and can source our own food. We can also keep our portions modest, particularly when it comes to fats and sugars, which are the ingredients causing the most health problems today.

The generalization that we are eating too much fat masks a further level of dietary imbalance that has been creeping in. Although all fats contain 9 calories per gram, not all fats are created equal. Hydrogenated fats, used in many processed foods, have a longer shelf life but can be harmful to the heart. Monounsaturated and polyunsaturated fats (such as olive oil) are recommended instead: these can help lower the risk of heart disease and provide vitamin E and other nutrients to help maintain our body's cells. Coconut oil (although it's not a good environmental choice for anyone living on the other side of the world to a coconut palm) is getting a great press now and is a good saturated fat for frying because it has a high smoke point. Reducing frying to a minimum and opting for a mixture of butter and olive oil when I do fry is my preferred healthy option.

The way the body is able to absorb the nutrients it needs from the food we eat is a source of great wonderment. It demonstrates a synergistic relationship between humans and their food sources over millions of years of evolution. As cooks, we need to be much more aware and careful that we are still getting the full variety of food we need, and that a wholesome understanding of nutrition underpins any promotion of food being grown, manufactured and sold for profit.

Variety is, indeed, the key to our continuing good health: the diverse elements that make up our total nutritional intake have always been spread over many different foodstuffs, as well as including diverse parts of 'whole' foods from skin to kernel. Now, more than ever, as goodness is pared away, or mixed and disguised in different forms and often over processed, we need to reach out for a variety of foods to make up for possible deficits. We need to secure this variety to create a colourful palette of food giving us the full range of nutrients needed for health.

# IN PRAISE OF NUTRITION

The classic metaphor that describes our body as our 'temple' is not a bad one when it comes to developing a broad-sweep appreciation of nutrition. In this temple, light shines through the windows as sunshine onto our skin synthesizing vitamin D – essential for bone health. Into the sacred inner space come all manner of nutrient 'people', bringing much-needed things in terms of praise, songs, good intentions, forgiveness, the wish to be loyal, to bond, to promote peace and a long life, to move through the rites of passage that punctuate our life from birth to death, and to facilitate this. The elements of nutrition are sifted or uplifted by our amazing body-temple, and what is required is assimilated into our body to build our health. The heightened sense of belonging that can be experienced during any communion can be likened to the effective and beneficial assimilation of good nutrition.

# Flexibility

Even when we agree about what is best for us to eat, it is important to keep flexible. Sometimes circumstances require and allow a bit of deviation from the desirable.

Being flexible is much easier when we experience the Buddhist teaching of 'non attachment' as a source of empowerment. 'You only lose what you cling to,' is how the Buddha put it. As soon as we dig deeper and find the ultimate source of motivation – love – there is really no need to cling to a particular way of doing things against all odds. As the Dalai Lama once remarked: 'Most of our troubles are due to our passionate desire for and attachment to things that we misapprehend as enduring entities.'

It isn't that we want to become indifferent and not care about the way things are. Flexibility means being prepared to think fresh, act fresh, and break habits. It means not allowing one particular thought to pre-empt our every action and take control of our behaviour, like an addiction.

## APPRECIATING ALTERNATIVES

So, if I cannot find organic food to cook, if I cannot get the balance of omega 3 and omega 6 fatty acids just right, or include a variety of fresh vegetables, nuts, and wholegrains on my plate for every meal, then I still take joy in knowing there is, and has always been, an alternative path. Not every day offers perfect nutrition, and to experience anxiety about the imperfection of yesterday's nutrition, or to refuse nutrition because it isn't the ideal, would only make things worse. Of course, it is sad that good, wise food is not always on our doorstep but it would be sadder to give up and turn away from any food. It would be sad, too, to decline a moment of earnest sharing. Rather, have confidence in your body's resilience and be part of the world as it is. Embrace this very moment as your opportunity for forward movement: you are part of the rippling river of change that brings vitality to life, just as food brings vitality to our bodies.

Being flexible has a lot to do with playfulness and not getting stuck in a rut that might be leading us to a very unproductive end. Opportunities to 'make believe' and dabble with alternative scenarios that make us laugh and behave differently may seem like no more than a game but in reality there is a hidden survival advantage that lies behind this engagement. Play allows us to rehearse different ways of being in a safe space that doesn't force us to abandon our usual life strategy. Because we think we are just playing, our guard is dropped and we find ourselves able to practise changing our mind – which is in reality not easy at all.

The ingredients we choose to cook, as well as who we cook for, provide a rich ground for playing with what's possible and opening up the arena of adaptability in a very experimental way. I was once invited to a small tea party to celebrate the birth of a Syrian baby, and was intrigued to taste all the unfamiliar spices in the carefully prepared foods. Such cross-cultural experiences and celebrations often offer the opportunity to flex beyond our usual or preferred eating patterns. Likewise, curious dishes derived from foraged ingredients have often taken me by surprise and seriously challenged my flexibility quotient. For example, a wonderful herbalist, Frank Cook, who studied at Schumacher College where I work used to like preparing lasagne using the dock leaves that grew on the lawn. Convinced that dock must be poisonous to humans (as well as guinea pigs and cows) I questioned him in some depth and did some of my own research. Finally convinced that it was entirely safe, I took a bite – and, yes, his dock lasagne was quite delicious.

Another unusual food item I have yet to taste but am delighted to know exists is chutney made from Japanese knotweed. This species is normally associated more with house sales falling through than culinary endeavour, since its roots are highly invasive and can seriously damage the foundations of properties. Perhaps the mindful lesson here is that willingness to experience new things smooths the path of transformation: it cultivates a way of being that opens us to seeing benefits, where before we might have kept our mind closed and dug ourselves into a hole.

# Celebration

Celebration reflects the importance of sharing and honouring ourselves and others who make up our lives, as well as the natural rhythms that mark our passage through this world, from birth to old age, spring to winter.

Birthday cakes, community feast days, the marking of the seasons with special meals: all are occasions when people gather together around food, reaffirming their bond to one another. Often the foods we have grown up experiencing on such occasions are flavours and recipes we will remember for life: vehicles for rekindling a positive experience of time spent with other people.

Almost every culture and every religion has special food associated with its feast days. Sometimes these are chosen for their direct association with certain historical events. Making and serving these foods thus provides a trigger for retelling stories that conjure up formative moments in the evolution of the knowledge and customs embodied by a group. For example, the Jewish festival of Hanukkah, the festival of lights, goes back almost 2,400 years and celebrates the rededication of the Holy Temple in Jerusalem after an invading army had damaged it. People cleaned the temple but found they did not have enough sacred oil to keep the candles burning for more than one night. Miraculously the candles continued to burn for eight days – enough time for more oil to be prepared. In recognition of the role of the oil, food eaten at Hanukkah is often fried. The Festival of Eid that comes at the end Ramadan marks the breaking of a month of fasting. Typically Eid al-Fitr includes lots of sweet foods, which give an energy boost and a sense of pleasure, but because Muslims are spread across the globe the typical food varies from place to place (though all will be halal), and dates are often included as a reminder of the Prophet Muhammad's original fast-breaking snack. In eating these foods, celebrants take into their very bodies the taste of their ancestors' trials and triumphs.

The Christian festivals of Christmas and Easter are also celebrated in many very different countries and climates with a fairly common food formula being used for at least the main course, where some kind of large roasted bird is typically served. What was appropriate for a northern winter feast that brought people together to share food in times of scarcity might not seem quite the right menu for a hot climate, yet I have heard of Australians celebrating Christmas in the sweltering heat and bringing out a steaming plum pudding alongside a pavlova. Possibly serving the traditional pud brought back fond memories of their country of origin to families who had emigrated, a moment of mindfulness of roots transcending everyday practicalities.

As well as the special foods that mark annual celebrations, there are the favourite foods that we choose to celebrate a very special achievement or event, something that doesn't happen every year. I was once asked to make a cake to celebrate the first anniversary of the 'transition' movement in Totnes, Devon, where I live. Totnes was the first of a growing number of communities to use the name 'transition town' as part of an international network of grassroots initiatives that aim to increase self-sufficiency, reduce our environmental impact and provide local economic stability. Later I was asked to provide a basic cake recipe for their network website. Transition Network's founder, Rob Hopkins, explained that he felt making a cake was a great way to celebrate the many landmark occasions that communities achieve when people come together to build local resilience. This could be the planting of an orchard of nut trees, the launch of a local currency, or equipping a street of houses with solar panels. Cakes are high calorie and sweet: delicious and more-ish, but definitely not foods we want to be eating every day. Because of this, we carve them up small and share them out between lots of people, and we can decorate them beautifully to echo the achievement we are celebrating.

The actual preparation and cooking of celebration food is usually part of the equation that brings people together, a kind of prequel to the event. Indeed, you could say that the careful planning and sharing out of cooking tasks is where the celebration really begins. Celebration is about doing things together and creating mutual acknowledgement, and food helps to anchor this. Because eating is a daily activity we all engage in, marrying food with celebration, and celebration with food, makes room in our lives for both.

In foregoing celebration and the making of special foods for such events, we may be missing out on a very life affirming activity – something that helps us make sense of who we are as living members of our diverse Earth community. So when we do engage in celebratory occasions, let's always take a moment to step back and really enjoy reflecting on the positives of how this joining moment has made us feel.

# Are We
# What We Eat?

The example of veganism provides an analytical and empathic pathway for the consideration of many ethical aspects of food and farming.

Parents are apt to tell greedy children that they will turn into any food they start to gorge upon: 'If you eat any more carrots, you'll go orange and turn into a carrot!' Biologically speaking, of course, it isn't possible. However, the recurrence of the idea betrays a certain universal anxiety and acknowledgement that there is an intimate connection between what we eat and who we become. This is far from just a game; rather, it shows an archetypal thought tendency concerning the nature of transformation that influences us all. Because of this, the 'we are what we eat' notion can be applied constructively to help us build awareness about how we impact our world and the people around us.

Nowhere is the concept of food's influence on character more apparent than in the contrast between meat-based and plant-based diets. In India, for instance, the ancient mind-body health system Ayurveda identifies categories of food based on how they both affect and reflect the human being at whatever stage of spiritual development they are at, identifying the most spiritual diet (known as Sattvic) as fruits, grains, vegetables, seeds, milk, yogurt and honey. The Rajasic category contains more stimulating foods such as fresh meat, wine, spices, garlic, onions, eggs and sweet foods, thought to encourage competitive, aggressive and sensual behaviour, while the final category, Tamasic, which includes fermented, decayed, decomposed, overcooked or reheated food with little life force left in them, is associated with darkness, inertia and disease.

Interestingly, as long ago as the time of the ancient Greeks, the historian Herodotus (c. 484–424 BCE) observed a correlation between meat eating and aggressive behaviour, while noting that cultures whose nutrition was mainly plant-based were occupied with more spiritual pursuits. This view was echoed in the early twentieth century by philosopher and author Rudolf Steiner, who established the practice of biodynamic agriculture, one of the first organic agricultural movements.

I am not a vegan but the more I read about mass factory farming and plunder of animals for food, the more I feel that my avoidance of industrial dairy produce as well as meat and fish in my diet is an ethically correct decision. In addition, the arguments for veganism lead me to question whether I should dim the light of dairy in my diet: dairy farming has an enormous impact on the environment and accounts for four per cent of the world's total greenhouse gas emissions. Thirty per cent of the Earth's land mass is used to grow crops to feed animals or graze them, and a meat-eater's diet requires on average seventeen times more land, fourteen times more water and at least ten times more energy than a vegetarian's or vegan's diet. A vegetarian has half the food-related carbon footprint of a meat eater and a vegan still less. Becoming vegan reduces your carbon footprint by, on average, 1.5 tons of carbon dioxide a year.

The question is, how do we hold the tension between ideal and reality? Arguments for veganism are very emotive, and we need to look beyond any knee-jerk reactions and employ a critical analysis from a holistic perspective when considering whether this is an appropriate and sustainable pathway for us (or the global population) to tread. We need to ask questions about alternatives. Can animal welfare be improved dramatically through the adoption of small-scale organic farming systems, such that these could create the context for a rich and fulfilling life for animals, given that they, like us, will die at some point anyway? Can our complex nutritional (as opposed to just calorific) needs be met through a vegan diet, and, if so, how? What would become of the domestic animal kingdom and our relationship to it if everyone changed to a vegan diet? How would we build an interface between animals and humans into such a society – and, by contrast, does a classic 'food chain' dependency have benefits for both animals and humans in terms of encouraging shared resources and, dare I say, friendship?

However far you may choose to tread along the path to veganism, one thing all the evidence points to is that our Western diet has become unhealthily protein-heavy, reflecting an overloaded consumption of animal protein. Going back to our starting point, future generations of parents might then be telling salutary tales not of children who turned orange through eating too many carrots, but of greedy ancestors who turned into 'beef burgers' through eating too much meat. Far worse than becoming orange, these meat-people could no longer see the difference between peace and war. The triumph would be in knowing this time had passed and that we were no longer in any danger of embodying such 'Tamasic' negativity.

# Thinking About
# Gluten & Sugar

The antagonists of conscious cooking are hybridization, accelerated factory methods and food monoculture. Can our food be too sweet – and can we?

Too much animal protein isn't the only dietary trend causing health problems today. Hand-in-hand with the mass production of food has come the need to create food that travels and stores well. When we eat food 'second hand' because it came ready-cooked from a shop rather than from our own oven, it has to make up in deliciousness what it lacks in freshness and the tempting aromas that comes with this. A little more salt and a lot more sugar are great ways to improve shelf life and make food more-ish, even when the natural fresh flavour is lost.

With respect to 'our daily bread', speeded-up industrial methods for making squidgy loaves of additive-rich sliced bread by the truckload seem to have coincided with an increased incidence of gluten intolerance. However, many people who thought they had a gluten or wheat allergy when they consumed mass-produced bread are now discovering that they can eat sourdough and other traditionally made loaves without any digestive problems. (The long, slow fermentation process needed to make sourdough, which follows on from using a natural leaven, makes sourdough easier to digest than the quickly produced yeasted bread made with over-hybridized wheat flour.) The revival of artisan bread-making across the world is at the forefront of a new consciousness about food preparation and the value of taking time to make food in the best way.

While gluten intolerance is a continuing problem for sufferers, the increase of sugar in our diet has possibly more extreme and widespread consequences. The medical conditions associated with excessive sugar consumption include diabetes type II, obesity, inflammation and metabolic syndrome. The recommendation of the American Heart Association is for most women to eat no more than 100 calories of sugar (6 teaspoons or 25g) per day and for men to consume no more than 150 calories (about 9 teaspoons or 36g) per day, which is at odds with the spiralling increase in sugar consumption seen in many countries as diets become more globalized. Much of the sugar we consume is 'hidden' in processed food but it nonetheless needs to fall within the total recommended amount for optimal health to be obtained.

The answer, though, is not to switch to artificial sweeteners, which can be carcinogenic and do nothing to retrain our love of sweetness; in fact they can have the opposite effect and increase our cravings because they do not even quench our limited need for the energy that sweetness should bring. Above all, banish sugary drinks from your fridge: high-fructose corn syrup in fizzy drinks is one of the biggest enemies to health in the world today. Grabbed on a daily basis, they bring only empty calories and the risk of tooth decay and obesity.

## LESS IS MORE

Although our taste for sugar seems to have escalated, the good thing is that we can also retrain our tastebuds to crave it less. This is a very worthwhile mindful practice, which involves gradually reducing the amount of sugar we consume almost by habit – for example, halving the sugar in our coffee or tea (if we use it), cutting down the sugar in our baking by a third, and reducing the sugar on our breakfast cereal. This is just phase one; the next step is to reduce the sugar a little more and perhaps replace sugar on our cereal or in cakes and desserts with a natural source of sweetness such as bananas, dates or other fresh fruit. It is amazing how the sweetness inherent in most foods begins to be detected and appreciated more and more.

Of course, natural sugars are also full of calories, so replacing sugar with honey or molasses will not bring about the desired effect of reducing your daily sugar consumption. However, within your daily allowance of sugar, enjoying sweetness in its most natural and 'whole' state will optimize the nutritional benefits. For example, by choosing an orange over a glass of orange juice, the whole fruit will give you just half your allowance of sugar, plus valuable fibre and other nutrients. In comparison, a glass of orange juice gives fewer nutrients and a full daily dose of sugar in one go – so there is less scope for enhancing your day with other sweet treats, be they a teaspoon of honey or jam on your bread, a juicy apple, or a few dried figs.

When thinking about sweetness imagine a smile – natural, warming and bright. Smiles that never stop or seem glued to people's faces quickly lose their charm. Likewise a diet of unending sweetness quickly loses its sense of 'gift' and begins to betray a ferment of underlying decay (which such a diet could indeed lead to). What no longer feels wholesome or moderated quickly loses its appeal: addiction is not the same as enjoyment.

# Treading the
# Sure-footed Path
## of Organic Farming

Organic farming provides a valuable tool for ensuring we are actively nurturing our own well-being as well as that of our environment and the creatures it embraces.

For thousands of years humans farmed organically. Resilient food systems were evolved, including agro-ecological systems, such as forest gardening. It was only after the industrial revolution that alternative methods began to develop, which included mechanization and the use of synthetic pesticides and fertilizers. Landmarks in the birth of modern industrialized agricultural systems were the invention of the tractor and the synthesis of nitrogen fertilizer in the mid-nineteenth century. The urgent view that we needed to increase production to feed an exploding population began to influence farming methods. As a consequence, animal welfare and environmental sustainability began to fall by the wayside.

Early in the twentieth century a few visionaries began to question the virtues of the new modern farming techniques and to favourably re-evaluate traditional agricultural methods that emphasized sustainability by means of a holistic and ecologically balanced approach. This was the dawn of organic farming for the modern era.

Despite growing awareness of the critical role of the soil, intensive practices continued to evolve. Two chemicals developed during the Second World War were applied to agriculture: ammonium nitrate, used in munitions, became an abundantly cheap source of nitrogen, and DDT, which had been used to control disease-carrying insects around troops, became a general insecticide, widely used on crops and in gardens. At the same time, larger-scale machinery allowed farmers to work bigger areas of land single-handedly, and miles of hedgerows were grubbed up – their value in preventing soil erosion and providing a habitat for wildlife was lost.

In the 1940s all talk was of the 'Green Revolution': a campaign to increase agricultural production and feed the world. For two decades, the focus was on developing high-yielding strains of cereal grains, chemically controlling pests and diseases, large-scale irrigation projects and significant mechanization of agriculture.

Only with the publication of American conservationist Rachel Carson's book *Silent Spring* in 1962 did the real dangers of using chemicals begin to be taken seriously. Her revelations about the effects of the indiscriminate use of pesticides were heard throughout the world, and led to the banning of DDT in the USA in 1972. This marked a turning point for the environmental movement and a renewed interest in organic farming.

In terms of animal welfare, the benefits of organic farming are well established. Livestock raised under organic certified standards must be free to range, fed quality food and must experience good living conditions and transportation. They must be treated compassionately and have their lives ended humanely. Because organically raised animals are not confined indoors or forced to gain weight too quickly, they experience less stress and less disease – meaning they require fewer drugs or antibiotics, which makes them healthier to eat.

The link between organic food and good health might seem obvious, perhaps indisputably so, but it hasn't been immediately easy to demonstrate. There is now, however, evidence that organic food, whether animal or vegetable, contains fewer or no pesticide residues, less harmful cadmium, and more nutrients, including significantly more omega 3s and anti-oxidants. Furthermore, because use of antibiotics is restricted, organic produce is not implicated in the public health crisis surrounding the development of antibiotic resistant strains of bacteria or the possible links between pesticide residues in our food and abnormal development of the brain in unborn babies.

Many people consider organic food to be too costly but as a society, once we see food as preventative medicine, it seems a price worth paying. If governments stopped subsidizing non-organic food and gave tax incentives to encourage organic farming, the cost difference would narrow, and our health, and that of the Earth, would benefit. Our land needs to be nurtured and cherished for what it provides. After all, the concept of the living soil is fundamental to any understanding of organic farming. You need only walk in a field, forest or garden and feel the soil underfoot to know that this is a dynamic substance that is life and gives life. If you are stuck indoors, reach for a plant pot on your window sill and feel the sense of potency and magic in the unassuming brown earth. Soil lives under our feet, an earth-skin of minerals, air, clay, water and decomposing life, a home to earthworms, beetles, moles, plant roots, fungi, insect larvae, bacteria and many other wonderful organisms. It is a fertile domain of organic matter where life and death merge creatively.

# Reasoning with
# Seasoning

There is no doubt that freshly harvested vegetables ripple with flavour, colour and life. When they arrive straight from the garden and into the arms of a waiting chef, we begin a co-creative journey that honours the work of the gardeners over many months. More than this, it honours the potential these unique plants possess – of which 'becoming food' is just one strand in their evolution. The same is true of everything else we eat: eggs, flesh and dairy. In a sense we are the hijackers of the substance of others but there is nothing inherently wrong in this. Once we accept this as life's modus operandi, we just need to make sure we negotiate our survival with maximum respect for all life.

We are all part of the same interconnected web of life where food begets food, just as life begets life.

So when we begin our journey of working with the food we cook, our aim is to simply do the best we can in terms of developing and complementing the natural flavours inherent in the ingredients. There are a few simple guidelines that can be relied upon to deliver the best results, and these begin with the time-honoured magic of a humble pinch of salt.

Both sea salt and rock salt are naturally occurring soluble minerals that have been found and enjoyed by humans and animals right from the earliest times. It is estimated that we each need a dose of 6g (a teaspoon) of salt every day to function properly. Used in cooking, a little goes a long way, and we do not need to be too timid: as most recipes advise, salt is something that needs to be added 'to taste'. Add a little to begin with and sample, then add a little more until the flavour of the salt brings out the flavours of the ingredients brightly but does not dominate them. Sometimes a squeeze of fresh lemon performs a similar miracle. A friend of mine, Tara, wanted to call her new restaurant 'The Salt' because, as she explained: 'Salt is the ingredient that brings everything together when you cook – and I want my cafe to bring everybody together to eat and enjoy good food.'

## MORE THAN SIMPLY SALT

Alongside salt, pepper is the next classic of seasoning, and what is important to remember is that using freshly ground black pepper makes all the difference. Like all spices, peppercorns possess essential oils that evaporate quickly, so if you grind them yourself, you will find a far more flavourful and aromatic addition that enhances not only the food you cook but your whole kitchen. Pre-ground spices are so convenient that we ignore the fact that they are probably stale but once we get into the habit of grinding our own spices, it makes such a subtle and uplifting difference that you won't go back.

## THE ART OF SEASONING

When it comes to considering how much pepper or spice to add to your menu, you will need to be your own judge. If you are trying to create a spicy menu typical of a particular national cuisine, you may want the seasoning to be quite dominant; however, if you simply want them to complement freshly grown organic vegetables, it is advisable to hold back. Add a few spices at the beginning of your cooking along with the oils, and allow time for their flavour to develop: oils help to carry the flavour of food. Halfway through cooking, taste and add more seasoning if needed; never forget to keep sampling your food as you cook it – especially when using spices. We need to keep tasting the food we cook to keep in touch with how those tastes are developing as they transform in the depths of a bubbling stew pot on the hob or in the oven. This intimacy between the cook and the cooked is always fruitful when it comes to developing depth of flavour, or for realizing our own unique food signature as a chef.

Another key thing to remember when it comes to mastering the art of seasoning is that some condiments are best added at different stages. Dried herbs, for example, need to be added at the beginning of cooking so they have more time to revive and for their flavours to come out. Fresh herbs, in contrast, can be used more lavishly and should be added at the end of cooking where their vibrant flavour, brighter colours and volatile oils will give much more liveliness and aroma to the dish – aspects which would be impaired by over-cooking. Recognizing what in our lives needs to be treated with delicacy and immediacy on the one hand, and what responds to being given time for gentle emergence on the other, is something we can reflect on as we cook – and as we reason with our seasoning.

# Mindful Eating,
## Mindful Mealtimes

Food is too important to be rushed so let's make a conscious decision to set aside our mealtimes to truly savour and appreciate it. We may then be more deeply nourished by it and wrapped in an uplifting sense of gratitude for all it represents.

When the moment for a meal arrives, there comes an opportunity to celebrate the sustaining wonder of replenishment in a very direct way. Even before the meal has begun, much work and thought has gone into creating the food we eat, from growing, harvesting, transporting, shopping to careful cooking. All these aspects can be brought into focus when we choose to make our mealtimes mindful.

A meal is almost always a source of natural and frequent joy. For food not to bring joy it needs to be either very bad, or the eater unwell in some way that impoverishes their normal instinctual delight. The general robustness of our love of food and the usual frequency of mealtimes make breakfast, lunch or supper perfect moments to practise mindfulness. Mindful eating could become a regular thing, or something you do once a day – or perhaps just for ten minutes now and then.

To begin with, make sure that you have set aside a quiet, undisturbed place in which to enjoy your meal. If you are sharing the experience with other people, then make sure that there is a common agreement supporting your attention to your food, and that you are following the same guiding principles, which usually includes observing silence.

As you sit down to eat, set aside all your electronic paraphernalia (if you have it – many nowadays live by it). No ear plugs feeding you with music or news.

Mobile turned off. Kitchen TV, off. Sensory overload, off. The only paraphernalia you will need for this exercise is a plate to hold your food and some kind of utensil to eat it with, be it knife, fork, spoon, chopsticks, or your own nice clean fingers.

If you are serving yourself, be mindful of the portions you take. Think not just of a good nutritional balance as you heap one dish then another onto your plate but of the visual arrangement. Notice how one dish complements another. Enjoy the colours, sometimes matching and muted, other times striking with dramatic contrasts of colour: red, white, green, or saffron yellow. So much creativity in nature and in cooking brings this to us.

As you pause for a moment before beginning to eat, take in the aromas of the food as they waft up to your nose. What herbs, spices, flavours do these speak of? Let your mind dwell on the provenance of the food, thinking of and thanking the gardeners and cooks who made this food what it is. You might also like to thank or think of the forces in nature that have been present in the evolution of these foods over thousands of years: the sun, the soil, the rain. Think of the journeys the food has taken to arrive on your plate.

When you lift your first morsel of food to your lips, allow it to rest longer in your mouth. Chew it well – sometimes 20–30 chews are recommended per mouthful. This allows the flavour to swim into your mouth and be tasted and appreciated more deeply. It also allows the digestive juices in your saliva to coat the food more intricately, beginning to break it down and aiding the process of digestion. The custom of chewing well is something that we often lose sight of in our hurry to gulp down fast food at a bus stop, yet it is a real aid to health, and something we can all practise without any cost. Make this first mouthful the model as you eat up the rest of your food. Eat slowly, enjoying and appreciating the food. Tune into the taste and texture and the way each morsel transforms in your mouth. As you swallow, feel it travelling into your body and becoming part of your strength, no longer a separate entity but part of your very being.

Between mouthfuls, put down your utensils and allow your hands to relax so you can concentrate on the sensations in your mouth. Be in no hurry to take another bite before the first is finished. In this way we avoid over-eating, which often comes from rushing our food and denying our body-mind the time and respect it needs to register satiation.

Mindful eating is an exercise not only in reaffirming the simple satisfaction of mealtimes, it also provides an opportunity to engage in gratefulness, which is an attitude to life that has been shown to promote greater happiness. Rather than focusing on what we have not, we are thankful for what we have. The practice of appreciation for what we eat can be extended beyond mealtimes – for example, when out walking in nature we might sit down for a moment of rest and enjoy eating some tasty berries, slowly savouring the fresh juices on our tongue.

# Lifting the Lid on
# **Superfoods**

Are there really such things as superfoods? What does 'super' mean, anyway? And what does it truly mean for food to be 'whole'?

The label 'superfood' is increasingly used to promote certain uncommon diets or ingredients that will (in theory) bring enormous health benefits when included as part of our daily intake. At its best, a so-called superfood identifies produce that is nutritionally dense: acai berries, wheatgrass and goji berries have all been hailed as ways to eat ourselves healthy. In part, the term represents a great new explosion of niche foods, often sold as supplements. These typically are sold under the banner of 'superfood' and wave a very large price ticket as a flag, making us think they must be something really special and worth paying for.

There is in fact no official definition of a 'superfood', and the European Union has banned health claims on packages unless substantiated by scientific evidence. This hasn't stopped the food industry trying to persuade us that so-called superfoods can slow down the ageing process, improve intelligence, lift depression – and they have the money to pay scientists to find something that they can parade as 'proof' for this. Often, the deceit comes in, not because a single food does not have some special properties, but because these special ingredients are usually only present in a fairly small way and would never be found in the quantities needed to make any real difference when taken in their food state.

What our earlier ponderings on organics have shown us is that food is already 'super' if we just let it be as natural as possible. You will, for example, find antioxidants in their plenty in fresh fruit and vegetables, as well as in some delicious extras, such as dark chocolate, cranberries, pecan nuts and kidney beans. Rather than adding anything to food either during its growth or its preparation, we need to stop doing unnecessary stuff to food and let it live up to its own nutritional potential. We also need to cut back on nutrition-depleting activities like shipping food around the globe, peeling wholefoods, and processing and preserving food in ways that detract from rather than enhance their health benefits.

Once we reset the parameters of what could justifiably be called a 'super' food in accordance with these guidelines, there is no reason why we shouldn't have the confidence to call, say, beetroot or kale or sauerkraut a 'super' food. In fact, any organic whole food can become the 'superfood' we need at a particular moment if it possesses the nutritional bonanza we require and we have prepared it in such a way that this can be passed on to us beneficially. What's unlikely, however, is that one food is going to provide a cure for all our problems, because what really counts is variety and wholeness.

Sauerkraut and kimchi are examples of traditional fermented food supplements that have stood the test of time. Humans have been fermenting food for millennia, in fact evidence goes back over 8,000 years. Long before there was any empirical evidence for how it worked, we had discovered the virtues of fermentation for preserving food, and were experiencing the heightened health benefits that come when we encourage the probiotic (literally 'for-life') microbes to flourish.

In reality, long before we 'discovered' fermentation, fermentation discovered us. This is to say that as animals, we are simply teaming with trillions of bacteria inside and outside our bodies – so many that they outnumber the cells in our bodies ten times over. The vast majority of these bacteria have taken up residence in our gut, where they perform minor miracles for us that make it possible to digest all sorts of food and fight off harmful pathogens.

What gives great hope for the health of the gut is the increasing popularity of fermented foods today.

Everywhere in the West, people are fermenting in their own kitchens. Fermentation classes are booking up overnight. So thirsty are people for this simple, powerful knowledge that the 're-wilding' of the gut through fermentation is creeping up the health agenda, dispelling the deadening effects of antibiotics on the inner landscape of our gut. In other parts of the world the knowledge and practice of making ferments has continued to be part of the food culture for millennia. Korea, for example, has the oldest history of eating ferments (kimchi being the most popular) and can also boast one of the lowest levels of cancer in the world.

The strong correlation shown between an ancient tradition of fermented foods and startlingly positive health benefits, with no negative side-effects, cannot fail to encourage us to meditate on the power of the tiny. Let's bear those microbes in mind. And let's meditate further on what happens when the power of the tiny is multiplied a trillion-fold and given the thumbs-up in our lives.

# Whittling Down
# Paraphernalia

---

Mindfulness involves achieving balance and finding ways to unclutter our lives, which include freeing up our kitchens and our dinner tables.

From high-tech blenders and mixing bowls to wooden spoons and silicone spatulas, or ceramic serving dishes spilling out of our kitchen cupboards and vases of flowers and electric pepper mills dominating our dinner tables, there is a serious danger that 'stuff' can start to take over our lives. Long before work surfaces disappear under our collection of paraphernalia and before we can barely move one thing without knocking over another, we need to ask ourselves, how much of this do we really need and how much is superfluous?

## IDENTIFYING THE ESSENTIALS

In a world where advertising is continually tempting us to buy this or that new gadget, it is very difficult to resist purchasing new things to experiment with. They may even arrive as gifts. Gadgets are a bit like the superfoods of the making world. They offer to do for us what we fancy we have difficulty doing for ourselves; indeed, advertising often plants the idea that we can't do things that we are quite capable of, or that we simply won't have time to try doing things we actually could make time for.

There is a great joy in reclaiming simplicity because it frees us up to be more creative with our own hands, and because it opens up a clear vista for appreciating what is important and setting our priorities straight. Once our priorities are straight in the kitchen, they also become clearer in the rest of our lives. In reality, there are very few things we absolutely need. A real sense of achievement will come from whittling down our possessions to find which are the truly essential ones.

For me, good-quality, lasting cooking equipment rates high on my list of essentials. I have three different sizes of saucepans (not non-stick), a frying pan, a rod blender, a few wooden spoons, a silicone spatula, a garlic crusher and a few sharp knives. But no electric lemon squeezer, no microwave, no electric steamer. Your list will be different from mine, depending on what you cook and the size of your family but for us all there is a serious danger of accumulating more and more, so for each new acquisition we need to think about where it will live and if there is something we could get rid of to make way for it. We also need to monitor our use of the new item to prove its usefulness.

When it comes to using microwaves to heat food, not only are there unresolved issues around food safety, but reheating ready meals seems quite unnecessary from a speed point of view. Simple and delicious meals can be prepared and cooked incredibly quickly on a conventional hob, and for me there is always a far greater joy in chopping and frying an onion than in removing cellophane from a plastic tray containing a pre-cooked meal and warming it up in two minutes. Oh, how I would miss the sound and smell of the sizzling onion and regret the extra plastic added to the planet's overflowing wastebin. Preparing food can free our minds from worrying thoughts, letting our hands take over, happy to work busily as only hands know best. This is precious time to become absorbed by a meditative task and provides an antidote to the rest of your busy day.

If we can constructively restrict our trappings, we will feel less trapped by them. Impediments restrict our freedom of movement and action, even in a kitchen. And when it comes to the dining table, we do not need the appurtenances of a banquet every day: just one glass per person is enough (and a tumbler for water). As for flowers, we should always favour local bounty over flown-in bouquets, and even then should consider saving their living beauty for special moments when we have time to really notice and contemplate their independent artistry and flamboyance of purpose.

Similarly, in the domain of mindfulness a crowd of thoughts can be much like a clutter of objects taking up unearned space. Just as some thoughts trigger negative emotions, objects attract dust and grime and block the way for new opportunities and new landscapes in which joy may flourish. In both cases, mental or physical impedimenta have perhaps become a waste of space. After a gentle acknowledgement of their presence, both can be helped on their way to the realm of recycling.

# Sharpening
## Our Knives and
# Our Lives

---

Cultivating precision in our lives requires care, regular attention and skill. When our knives are sharp we can chop mindfully, with far less risk of cutting ourselves – or unintentionally hurting others.

By recognizing and looking after our tools as if they were part of a daily meditation practice, they become an extension of ourselves and serve us better. They allow us to realize a greater potential and do more in the world. For a builder, it could be that a hammer, saw and drill are the most indispensable aids; for a doctor, it could be a thermometer and a stethoscope.

For a cook, however, it is perhaps a simple knife that is the most essential instrument. Often when new chefs are invited for an interview, they bring with them their favourite knife, carefully wrapped and sharpened. Many conversations about preferred kinds of knife are had in a working kitchen and chefs are happy to pay considerable sums, guarding their blades keenly and sharpening them with love.

## USING OUR HANDS

In almost all the examples of tools we can think of, the major connection point to the self is through our hands. It is our hands that provide the means of communicating the intentions of the mind to the tool and bringing it alive for us, making it our agent of change. Our hands learn to hold tools in just the right way to make them optimally effective, and hands also learn how to service them regularly – something which usually means using other tools in a special way to maintain, for example, the sharpness of the knife or to prevent rust developing.

Now, it might be considered that sharpness is not a mindful quality, but rather something associated with fierce battles, wars and killing. Indeed, as with many qualities, there is a shadow side to sharpness, so we need to consider carefully what it is all about.

The kind of sharpness I am interested in is an aid to precision. It offers a diamond-like edge that facilitates the swift division of one thing into many things. It works against 'stuckness', attachment and heaviness, allowing us to re-create the elements of the world to better fit our needs. Thus, a collection of vegetables once chopped up can be put into a pot and cooked into a stew. Sharpness is an agent of transformation – which is, after all, what cooking is about.

The opposite of sharpness is bluntness, which I have many times found to be a greater danger in the kitchen, as it can cause us to struggle with our chopping and sometimes slip. Knowing whether to expect a sharp or blunt knife is however the most important thing when it comes to safety: at Schumacher we always put up lots of warning signs in our kitchen when the knives have just been sharpened, and keep our sharpest blades under wraps. Likewise in life, we respond better when we come prepared for working with a particular kind of behaviour, whether its edge is keen or dull.

In the psychological domain, both bluntness and sharpness can be used to refer to an unpleasant manner. In both cases, lack of sympathy is likely to stem from an absence of wholeness or sense of inequality in the relationship: it is as if the person delivering the message hasn't learned to protect their knife-like qualities from others, or they choose not to.

Someone who is too sharp typically leaves the person they are addressing feeling wounded or put down. By contrast, good chefs are always careful about how they carry their tool, aware that it can cause damage to others if left in a sink, a drawer or anywhere its sharp edge may lead to an unwelcome encounter.

Bluntness also lacks delicacy, but is sometimes valued for its honesty. In a knife, it can be associated with dullness and delay rather than reluctance to consider feelings; however, it probably comes to the same thing. If you allow a blade to lose its edge, you are neglecting the needs of the person who will use it, limiting their power to work effectively.

A sharp knife works more easily and fluidly with our mood, allowing us to set the pace as we work. Sometimes I listen to the sound of experienced chefs at work, noticing that at one moment the work is so velvety, smooth and rolling that the only sound to be heard is the crunch of the vegetable as the knife slices through, never completely leaving the board. Other times the chef decides to bang his or her knife rhythmically at the end of each sequence of slicing. A carrot flies into twenty rings. Bang! Another carrot sliced into twenty-two rings. Bang! And so on. It is almost like a drummer or a percussionist at work: the chef is fully immersed and enjoying the activity. Such an energized approach flows harmoniously into the creation of the meal, pouring added liveliness into it.

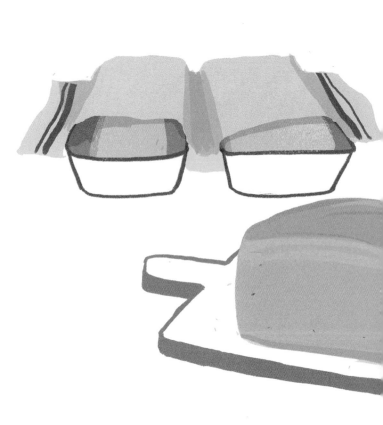

# Patience,
## the Most Important
# Ingredient of All

We need to be patient as well as swift when the moment is ripe, to make the best, fullest and most flavoursome food. Patience is an enlightened approach to life, born from deep understanding of how things work.

Standing over a hob stirring a bowl of milk and egg yolk suspended over simmering water . . . be patient! Wait for the custard to thicken gently. Turn down the heat so it doesn't boil. Make sure it will be perfectly smooth, not curdled or grainy. There is no need to rush: if you rush you risk spoiling everything.

Well, not quite everything – but in cooking there are some processes you just can't fast-track. You can't push an egg to poach to the perfect tacky-yolked consistency you want just because you have an appointment in three minutes, you're late and you're looking fiercely at the egg. If you want your food to taste the absolute best, you need to build the time it takes into every menu – and that is a lesson that fits us for life. Allow time to take time.

## PATIENCE REWARDED

Sometimes people ask me, 'How long does it take to make a loaf of bread?' They are concerned that making bread must be very time-consuming, and they think they could never fit it into their busy lives. However, once put in motion, the process of making bread demands just fleeting attention over the course of a day. It is the quality of the attention that counts – and the length of time between the moments of attention.

When making artisan bread, patience will be greatly rewarded as the fermentation takes hold and the natural yeasts feeding off the carbohydrate in the flour give off carbon dioxide that creates bubbles in the dough, which are held in place by the gluten in the wheat. A slow process described as 'pre-digestion' takes place, which makes the bread better for our health, and more easy to digest than the quickly made yeasted breads that have been commercially developed for mass-production. By contrast, for our own leavened bread, all we have done is a little mixing and then an occasional gentle kneading, and finally some shaping. Then, as if the rising dough is dancing in step with the warmth and humidity of the day, a moment will come when the bread is perfectly risen, ready to slide into a hot oven and be baked. More patience is then required as you wait and observe what is usually a regular baking time. When the bread is ready, take it out, tap it, squeeze it, let it air on a baking tray – and try to be patient. Don't start cutting it up while it is still steaming and hot.

At this point you actually could spoil everything: you could squash your bread, deflating all those time-grown, oven-seared, butter-hugging bubbles.

Breadmaking is one of countless examples that cooking offers that teach the importance of waiting. Don't undercook a cake, otherwise it will still be gooey in the middle when you cut it. Don't wander away from the stove and allow your green vegetables to overcook, or they will turn a dull khaki, taste mushy and boring, and lose their nutritional value. Don't undercook your rice, or you may break your teeth on it. Everywhere in cooking there are opportunities for using your judgement and exercising patience.

Patience is also an essential requirement when it comes to selecting choice ingredients. Thus, we need to wait for the ripening of the tomatoes on the vines before we pick them, just as much as we need to wait for them to braise in the oven until they are just as succulent and juicy as we want: perhaps a little browned, but not too much.

The 1980s witnessed the birth of the Slow Food movement in Italy, which can be seen as a reaction to the removal of patience from food. On the Spanish Steps in Rome a McDonald's burger joint was being opened. Sacrilege! Suddenly, people could simply go into a restaurant and order fast food that would be ready in five minutes because it was made from pre-prepared elements with a production line of people rushing to zoom it out to customers. What was happening? This event galvanized journalist Carlo Petrini into action, and it proved to be a catalyst to the forming of a movement that firmly puts the quality of food and the experience of eating first. Central to the Slow Food movement is the importance of preparing food using age-old, locally based production methods, together with the convivial social experience of sitting down at a table, often for hours at a time. None of this grabbing of chips and burgers to eat on the hoof! And so we see that patience and enjoyment are intimately linked in the book of fine dining.

# Thinking About
# Food Waste

Have we lost touch with our own food footprint?
Do we have the power to change step?

According to the global initiative SAVE FOOD,
a shocking one third of all food produced in the world
today for humans is lost or wasted. We're talking about
a staggering 1.3 billion metric tons. Even if a quarter
of this food could be saved, it would be enough to feed
870 million hungry people, which would make a huge
difference in a world where 795 million people are
estimated to suffer from chronic undernourishment
(this equates to one ninth of the world population). If
we could decrease our food waste, we would not only
put less pressure on scarce natural resources but reduce

the need to increase food production in order to meet the demands of a growing population. Not only will there be environmental and societal benefits; at a personal level, we will each have learned a lesson in 'joining the dots' in a world where the 'dots' have become so far apart that we frequently fail to see the bigger picture that we are a part of.

To begin with, do we have any idea how much food we eat over the course of a year? Every day we harvest or buy, prepare and eat food. We compost or throw out leftovers, go to bed, sleep, and hopefully wake refreshed and ready to start the new day. With a life so punctuated by beginnings and endings, in which we are held by what seems a comfortable diurnal rhythm, it's difficult to get a constructive sense of how much we eat, or what becomes of what we don't eat over the course of a week, let alone a year. Living a country life, we might once have seen our leftovers accumulating in a bucket for the pigs and chickens and had a sense of our accumulating waste. Nowadays, however, the evidence is whisked away. Similarly, we might have had the amount we gather to cook on a daily basis limited by how much was in the garden or how much money we had in our pockets, but nowadays we seem to be living in the midst of unbounded abundance. Being tempted by impulse buys in a supermarket, lack of planning and over-purchasing of food rank high among the reasons for food waste at the consumer end.

Looking at the statistics (including composted waste), food production per person is about 900kg (2000lb) a year in economically richer countries and about 460kg (1,022lb) per person in the economically poorer areas. By contrast, consumer food waste is about 95–115kg (211–255lb) a year in those richer countries, whereas it is only 6–11kg (13–24lb) per person in poorer regions. The difference is rather stark.

So what can we do to help? In developing countries, 40 per cent of losses happen at the point of harvest and processing, which could be helped by direct support of farmers and investment in appropriate technology.

But 40 per cent of food waste in the Western world is generated at the consumer end of the food supply chain, meaning there is a lot of scope for targeted educational campaigns and awareness building.

Sell-by dates, for instance, cause a lot of unnecessary waste, and there has been a lot of emphasis on revising these in the last few years, including introducing new techniques of heat-sensitive wrappings that show when food is actually going off rather than putting an estimated date on the packet. Increased awareness has also spurred an alternative food distribution system both officially and unofficially, often aimed at helping those who cannot afford shop prices. Thus raiding container bins and redistributing graded-out produce can be seen as mindful acts in which human creativity and kindness prevails in the face of bureaucratic blanket rules.

These and other programs have achieved considerable success, largely due to our own openness to change as soon as connections and consequences become apparent. Thus, moments of in-store education meet us at a time when we are quite receptive – perhaps waiting in a queue at the check-out so we don't feel our precious time is being wasted. Many or indeed most of us will also have felt the issue of accumulating waste, including food waste, niggling away at the back of our minds wanting us to do something about it. Being given effective strategies for buying, storing and cooking food less wastefully allow us to feel better about ourselves and what we are doing for our family and the planet.

It's not surprising, then, that education-based campaigns have managed to achieve significant decreases in household food waste, and the trend is continuing. With mindfulness, we can all be part of it.

# Seeing the
# **Perfect** in the
# Imperfect

What's more important: how food looks or how it tastes? Embracing the nutritional benefit of organic and misshapen fruit and vegetables is also about embracing the perfection of imperfection.

Bruised bananas, wonky veg and loving our leftovers all contribute to a lifestyle where we are in greater balance with our environment. A major cause of food waste is shops grading out 'ugly' fruit and vegetables, or catches of fish where up to half may be discarded for being the wrong size or species. Food waste campaigns around the world have focused on changing attitudes towards imperfect produce, and educating individuals and restaurants about its nutritional value, as well as finding alternative outlets for this produce. One example is a California-based company called Imperfect Produce, which sells its 'unattractive' goods at discounted rates, saving huge amounts of food, water and carbon dioxide.

Advertising panders to our childlike desire for perfection, and colludes with it. We may not realize that psychological complexes are being triggered that encourage unobtainable desires to swell into perceived, and sometimes desperate, needs. But we all have plenty of desires we are better off leaving as fleeting wishes, not dreams that have to manifest.

In short, the consumer culture manipulates us into thinking we should be perfect, and that perfection can be bought. Excuses for our excesses are forever being legitimized. Advertising offers us perfect solutions, over and over again. We accept propaganda's promises as legitimate, and then are disappointed, over and over again. This provides no bedrock for action, because we are inevitably and continually finding that reality does not live up to expectation, and the apathy that comes from repeatedly being let down doesn't breed the energy we need to harness and ride with change.

By contrast, the idea of embracing imperfection can be found in the Japanese philosophy called wabi-sabi, which accepts the three qualities of life that are found at the heart of Buddhist understanding whereby everything is considered to be impermanent, imperfect and incomplete. Instead of struggling with these realities, we can make peace with them. Thus the crooked carrots and bulbous pears become our teachers, and can be seen as heralds for the wabi-sabi aesthetic which includes asymmetry, roughness, simplicity and a modesty that brings with it a sense of intimacy.

It is perhaps easier to capture a sense of 'wabi-sabiness' in the look of a simple, unrefined tea bowl than in words. Thus the perfect imperfect bowl for a Japanese tea ceremony would proudly show the patina of age, evidenced by its wear and tear. Likewise, the deep golden, wrinkled apple that has been stored for several months, and bears a blemish where it was eaten by a wasp, has a greater fascination because of the story it tells and the life it has lived. It is also so deeply tasty: it will not last. And the bowl, eventually, will chip beyond repair.

The fact that nothing endures, nothing gets finished and nothing is ever perfect (including ourselves) meshes with the path of sustainability, because it lowers the bar of our reasonable expectations and brings them within the domain of reality. Working in the knowledge that everything keeps changing, that there is pain and there is boredom and that no quick purchase is going to whisk this away, is surprisingly empowering. It corresponds with our experience, so there is no disappointment. It's just *dukkha*, as Buddhism calls worldly discontent – but *dukkha* passes and we get on with it. It returns but we, understanding this is how life ticks, have compassion for all the suffering in the world, feel empathy with other sentient beings and engage in a practice of going forward harnessing change to make positive change.

In this light, global information and images on the crisis of waste should be taken as a wake-up call that inspires us to rein in our excess and become more aware of unconscious wasteful habits we may have developed. We are now well on the way to responding to this challenge and returning the old adage 'waste not want not' to the centre of a more 'joined-up' lifestyle. Our behaviour as consumers isn't the only thing that counts when it comes to reducing food waste, or waste generally but it is as consumers that we have the most power. We can reduce personal over-consumption, over-packaging and unnecessary use of energy. We can shrink our carbon footprint without any threat to our happiness once we realize happiness is nothing to do with ownership of stuff.

This means taking action is an inspiring place to begin the journey to sustainable sustenance. We'll make mistakes of course, and sometimes it will seem like an uphill struggle but once we see the perfect in the imperfect, all life is worth defending, and worth sending loving kindness out to in thought and word and deed.

# Embracing
# Thankfulness

Stepping into the mindful space of gratitude, blessing
our food at mealtimes is an expression of thankfulness
that happens the world over. Think of the casual rhyme
'*Rub-a-dub-dub, thanks for the grub!*'; the polite
Japanese phrase '*Itadakimasu*' ('I humbly receive');
or the Selkirk Grace of the Scots:

> *Some hae meat and canna eat,*
> *And some wad eat that want it;*
> *But we hae meat, and we can eat,*
> *Sae let the Lord be thankit;*

the Protestant refrain:

> *For what we are about to receive*
> *may the Lord make us truly thankful, Amen;*

the Islamic supplication:

*Allahumma barik lana fima razaqtana*
*waqina athaban-nar*

(O Allah! Bless the food You have provided us
and save us from the punishment of the hellfire);
and the Five Reflections of the Zen Buddhist tradition
that start with the words '*Gokan-no-ge*'. However we
express it, saying 'thank you' must be fulfilling some
kind of universal need or realization.

Even though saying 'grace' before beginning a meal
happens all over the globe, it isn't a habit that happens
in every family or at all times. Rather, it is something
that we do when we are able to take a moment for
conscientious reflection, often if we are part of a group,
if a particularly special or large meal has been prepared,
or if we ourselves are taking time to live attentively.

I wasn't brought up with a tradition of meal blessing,
except at lunchtime in my Church of England primary
school. Perhaps because of this, I now feel the value of
taking a moment to consciously appreciate the gift

of food more particularly. It doesn't seem automatic or habitual; rather, after a long morning of cooking, sometimes for 85–100 people, the moment of blessing is an opportunity to stand back and reflect on what has been achieved and thank all those involved: from gardeners, cooks, goats, chickens, cows to earthworms. It is a moment of putting everything into perspective and enjoying a quietness as we stand looking at the food we have created together. Sometimes it seems to me that each dish represents a busy thought that has spent the last two hours vying for my attention!

In this moment of awareness where cooks, washer-uppers and a handful of teachers, students and gardeners, stand looking at the wonderful feast that is the product of our morning's work, everything comes together. The demanding roast beetroot and Stilton salad that called for a bit more chilli is calm and shining; the lentil soup that argued for more blending is sitting comfortably waiting to give delicious nutrition to everyone; the green leaves that had to have all their caterpillars shaken out look bright and enticing. Fresh from the oven, the bread is voluptuous, smells tempting and is ready to be broken and shared. So for once, the menu-thoughts are set free from the mind of the cook that incubated them, and the cook is free from worrying over them.

Just as with our thoughts and emotions, food preparation is something that profits from a detached awareness. It is in the nature of being a chef that we are continually bombarded by deadlines: lunch at 1pm, supper at 6.30pm and so forth. Deadlines require careful organization if they are to be met successfully, and getting things done on time when anything backfires can easily become a cause of stress. The issue could be as simple as one of the team being ill and not showing up, or ten kilos of potatoes from the garden showing up but with slug holes in them, which requires double the preparation time. As with any other situation, mindfulness practice offers the opportunity to step outside the situation and observe it for what it is.

The miracle is that in doing so, rather than slowing everything down further, a space is usually created where calm enters, oiling the wheels of motion and allowing us to focus in a more detached and efficient way on manifesting our magnificent menu.

When we step back and put into perspective what we are doing, it is incredible. On a daily basis, we are transforming the bounty of our living Earth into not just palatable but deeply appetizing and attractive dishes of food. We are being given an opportunity to use our imagination and to share our culinary talents for the greater good.

When we bless our food, or thank God (or Mother Nature) for the gift of it, we are bringing to mind the continuing amazing force that fuels life and is life. We are voicing our appreciation of how lucky we are to be part of this continuum – and, as in the Selkirk blessing quoted on page 143, we are acknowledging that others may not be so lucky, which makes us all the more grateful.

# The Joy of
# Cooking

Let's welcome in the deep meditative pleasure of
cooking and being joyfully alive in the heart of our
homes. Feeling the empowerment that comes as we
create, improvise, share and engage in the sanity of
small tasks that bring balance to our day.

Back in 1931 when Irma Rombauer published the
very first edition of America's classic guide *The Joy of
Cooking*, there were very few gadgets to do the job for
us, electric or otherwise. Preparing food was still a quiet
activity, and the ingredients, although limited, were for
the main part wholesome and unsprayed. In fact, some
of the processes involved were just those that I would
recommend as meditative practices for a mindful cook

of today: for example, rubbing cooked vegetables or fruit through a sieve to create a purée rather than using a food processor, or making pastry and bread from scratch rather than buying them ready-made from the supermarket. The title chosen is itself revealing. For a tenacious widow who was trying to put her husband's recent death behind her, the decision to embark on the huge task of writing a cookbook that would become best friend to many American housewives shows that cooking itself is a great domain in which to find renewal.

As someone who was brought up in England, I reached for another encyclopedic cookbook called *Good Housekeeping* for my earliest childhood cooking lessons. The book had been one of my mother's wedding presents, and in its food-stained pages I found a comprehensive introduction to the art of cooking.

These manuals helped me cultivate the confidence to improvise from an early age. I was lucky that my mother and father (almost) never told me things weren't possible or kept too close an eye on me, so I was

free to make mistakes. I mixed up cakes with all the
joy I had once mixed up mud pies in the garden. In
fact, I remember once being found carrying eggs into
the garden to put in my mud pie – but that was a step
too far even for my parents, and I was fortunately not
allowed to complete the experiment!

While on the one hand I loved discovering recipes,
I also learned to begin making my own mixtures and
I slowly developed a clear sense of the parameters of
improvisation. Today, I always ask my chefs to practise
their improvisations at home first, and I do the same,
but I will risk serving untried new dishes which are a
variation on a familiar theme: it helps keep the menu
refreshed or dynamic. It is possible to 'imagine' taste
combinations with your tongue, and the more you cook
the better idea you will get about what tastes good
together. Many books give advice about what will go
with what but the more embodied learning comes
from working it out for yourself, particularly as
everyone's taste varies.

When you first start to improvise, try just changing one or two ingredients. Think about the kind of food you feel like eating or serving, as if you were an artist about to paint a landscape. Will I paint a sunset or a snowscape or a deep dark wood? Do I want the meal to be hot and spicy, or light and fragrant?

There is a joy that comes with using leftovers, which can feed into your culinary riff. Rather than just heating them, a few additions can transform them into something quite other and rather special; in fact, you could have invented a new recipe that is worth writing down!

Putting aside time to 'feed your freezer' also gives a great sense of achievement and joy. A very constructive free day can be spent cooking some of your favourite family dishes, cooling and packaging them, labelling them and freezing them for another time. Sometimes what I love about these defrosted menus is how the sense of the peace and achievement of the long gone day when I cooked the food comes flooding back to me as I reheat the dish and serve it up.

Even when a whole day is not available for the task, I enjoy doubling up what I cook to squirrel away a portion in my freezer – and I enjoy the opportunity of sharing some of this food with others, perhaps when they are very busy, or facing a time of stress.

And once all your cooking is done, there is the joy of 'washing the dishes to wash the dishes', which has been mentioned by the Buddhist monk and spiritual leader Thich Nhat Hanh on many occasions in his teachings and writings on the nature of being present for a task. We can enjoy the warmth of the foamy water on our hands and the engagement in the task of cleaning the dishes. Be there for the dishes and for the great joy of restoration that comes when we bring a task full cycle and return the laboratory that is our kitchen (or indeed anyone else's) to order and back to a more harmonious level of repose.

# The Final
## Garnish:
## Cultivating Simplicity

The perfect embellishment need only be minimal, yet it must speak with a strong, bright voice as a messenger for the greater and more complex whole.

The art of cooking realizes its potential when the food is devoured, and there are often several acts with many scenes to tantalize, draw us in and ultimately leave us satisfied. Every course offers an experience unique to itself, yet is also part of the whole that is the full menu. Typically, when cast as a banquet or feast, a meal can involve three or more courses, from a minimal hors d'oeuvre at the start through to a hearty main course, a dessert, cheeses and coffee or a liqueur at the end. The combination of courses differs from family to family and place to place, with some meals starting with a green salad and others bringing on a green salad before the dessert to freshen the palate. Within every course, each and every dish provides scope for decoration – so the art of garnishing becomes something we need to practise over and over again.

## GARNISH TO EMBELLISH

The perfect garnish works as an echo of the contents of the main dish it adorns. It should never be so elaborate as to completely disguise the dish it is supposed to amplify: rather, it offers a clue to what is inside. Alternatively, a garnish may simply provide a beautifying contrast, much as a rosette on top of a gift looks pretty but has no function. The use of a garnish that has no relationship to the contents of the dish may be important when, for example, a rather boring-looking brown paté or bean dip is being displayed, and a surround of green watercress helps to lift the appearance of the greyish food, making it more appetizing. Typically, garnishes are made from bright greens like fresh parsley, coriander and cucumber, or they may involve a twist of lemon which brings brightness of both taste and colour. Also lovely are garnishes of edible flowers like nasturtiums, marigolds and rose petals. These should also be kept minimal for maximum impact and contrast.

At times of abundance there is a need to rein in an over-use of flowers, thus preventing the surface of a green salad transforming into a veritable flower garden with barely a glimpse of leaf between the blossoms. Some flowers are better used and easier to eat when their petals are pulled off and mixed through a salad: marigold petals, for instance, provide an elegant dappling of orange, whereas the whole flower head makes a rather chewy mouthful. There are times, however, when a single flower is just the garnish that is required, and it is not a requisite that all embellishments are eaten; some may be left on the edge of the plate having served their purpose. Next stop the compost heap.

There is a sense in which a garnish can be seen as an expression of 'interbeing', to use a concept that is frequently returned to in the writings of Thich Nhat Hanh. Interbeing emphasizes the coexistence and interdependence of many different aspects of life. In an apple, for example, we not only feel the crunch of the white flesh against our teeth and taste the fresh tangy juices as they burst into our mouths; we see the work of the apple pickers and those who care for the orchard, we see the sheep grazing around the trees, and the sunshine and clouds and rain that have nourished the growth of the tree since a tiny seed; we see the stars and moon filtering through the dark sky every night, heralding the passing of the seasons, the years, and the decades.

All this we can see in an apple – and in a garnish, we can see another conversation. The garnish gives a clue to the dialogue the cook has entered into with the ingredients, holding some back to use later as decoration, while others have been carefully sautéd, blended, mixed and tasted. Before this they have been carefully sourced and grown, and perhaps, once ready, the food has been refrigerated, awaiting its debut on the table. Then, at the last moment, just before serving, the surface of the prepared food will be adorned with a flourish offered by the hand of the cook. This may take the form of a scattering of fresh herbs, a trail of blazing spices or a drizzle of oil, for all these will restore freshness and vitality to the surface of a food that has been lying in waiting.

The final garnish, the decoration on the food that makes it look that extra bit more beautiful, is like the secret message between the food and the cook. 'I love you – and everyone else will too! Farewell on your journey, and may you spread well-being and contentment.'

## DEDICATION

For my aunt, Laura Ponsonby, botanist, musician
and cook, who liked few things better than what she
called 'social cooking' with her family (both human
and feline) at Shulbrede Priory, West Sussex, and
who once served me an unforgettable slice of giant
puffball on the eve of a local election in Kensington.

## ACKNOWLEDGEMENTS

My thanks go to all those who have provided
inspiration for this little book: Wendy Cook for her
insights into human evolution and diet; Kaira Lingo
Jewel for her mindfulness teaching; Monica Perdoni,
commissioning editor at Leaping Hare Press, for
her joyful encouragement and Stephanie Evans
for her cheerful editing.